Science in Ancient Greece

α β

Kathlyn Gay

BLACK SEA

SEA OF
MARMARA

MACEDONIA

N

AEGEAN
SEA

ASIA MINOR

IONIAN
SEA

Athens

Miletus

Sparta

MEDITERRANEAN
SEA

Crete

0   150 km

0   100 mi

α   β ψ

Science in Ancient Greece

α β

Kathlyn Gay

Science of the Past

FRANKLIN WATTS

A Division of Grolier Publishing
New York • London • Hong Kong • Sydney
Danbury, Connecticut

Visit Franklin Watts on the Internet at: http://publishing.grolier.com

Photographs ©: Ancient Art & Architecture Collection: 12, 36, 42 (Ronald Sheridan), 17; Art Resource: 29 (Giraudon), 6, 10, 14, 24, 32 bottom, 38, 39, 47 (Erich Lessing); Christie's Images: 8, 19; e.t. archive: 13, 30, 50; National Library of Medicine: 44; North Wind Picture Archives: 9, 40; Photo Researchers: 16, 25, 33 (Jean-Loup Charmet), 57 (Hubertus Kanus), 21, 41, 48 (Science Photo Library); The Bridgeman Art Library International: 53, 56, cover; Tony Stone Images: 20; UPI/Corbis-Bettmann: 18, 22, 23, 32 top, 43, 45, 46, 49, 54, 58.

Maps created by XNR Productions Inc.

Illustrations by Drew Brook Cormack Associates

Library of Congress Cataloging-in-Publication Data

Gay, Kathlyn.
Science in ancient Greece / Kathlyn Gay. — Rev. ed.
p.   cm. — (Science of the past)
Includes bibliographical references and index.
Summary: Discusses the theories of ancient Greek philosopher-scientists such as Ptolemy, Pythagoras, Hippocrates, and Aristotle, and describes some of the scientific discoveries attributed to the Greeks and their impact on modern science.
ISBN 0-531-20357-3 (lib. bdg.)   0-531-15929-9 (pbk.)
1. Science—Greece—History—Juvenile literature.   2. Engineering—Greece—History—Juvenile literature.   3. Science, Ancient—Juvenile literature.   4. Scientists—Greece—Juvenile literature.   [1. Science—Greece—History.   2. Technology—Greece—History.   3. Scientists—Greece.   4. Philosophers—Greece.]   I. Title. II. Series.
Q127.G7G39   1998
509'.38—dc21
97-24029
CIP
AC

CONTENTS

chapter 1

The Story of Ancient Greece

α

β ψ

A Minoan sculpture shows a musician playing a stringed instrument called a lyre.

About 5,000 years ago, a great *civilization* arose on Crete, an island in the Mediterranean Sea. Crete lies south of what is now known as mainland Greece. The people who built this civilization called themselves Minoans. According to legend, they took their name from one of their early leaders—King Minos. Although the Minoans were not Greeks, many of the ideas that we attribute to the Greeks have their origins in Minoan culture.

The Greek mainland was settled by people from the north about 4,000 years ago. Today we call this group of people the Mycenaeans because their largest town was named Mycenae. The Mycenaeans were the first people to speak the Greek language. They developed a powerful culture, building splendid temples and mighty walled cities.

About 3,500 years ago, the Mycenaeans conquered the Minoans and adopted many features of Minoan culture. Just 300 years later, the Mycenaean civilization was destroyed. Many Mycenaeans fled to Asia Minor, taking their knowledge with them.

The people remaining in Greece now lived in small isolated villages. These communities were organized into independent city-states. Each city-state was ruled by a king, a dictator, or a group of wealthy families. As time passed, some city-states grew so large that they became over-crowded. As a result, about 2,700 years ago, Greek-speaking people began to move into Italy and the coastal areas of Asia Minor.

During the next several hundred years, city-states battled with one another for power and wealth. Each was like a separate nation with its own leader. While some leaders treated their citizens cruelly, others wanted to improve the quality of life for everyone. It was during this time that the concepts of *democracy* and individual freedom first arose.

The Greeks did not wage war only against one another. They were also forced to fight the armies of the quickly expanding Persian Empire. After many years of battling the Persian troops separately, the Greek city-states agreed to combine forces. By cooperating, the Greeks were able to defeat the Persians once and for all.

An artist's interpretation of Greek soldiers fighting

A scene from the great city of Sparta
in ancient Greece

The victory showed the Greeks what they could accomplish by
working together. Many city-states decided to unite with their neighbor-
ing city-states. But the Greeks were unable to set aside all their differ-
ences. Over time, two large powerful city-states—Athens and Sparta—
emerged. Athens became Greece's artistic and cultural center. Many of

ancient Greece's greatest philosophers, scientists, writers, and artists lived in Athens during this Golden Age. The Spartans were more interested in building strong armies than in thinking about or exploring the world around them.

About 2,400 years ago, a great war broke out between Athens and Sparta. Although the Spartans won that war, it was not long before they

A painting on a 2,600-year-old Greek vase
shows warriors at battle

were defeated by the Macedonians, a group of people who lived north of Greece.

The Macedonians allowed the Greeks to live much as they had before the invasion. They were so impressed by the accomplishments of the Greeks that they adopted many Greek ideas. As they conquered parts of the Persian Empire, the Macedonians spread these ideas to Egypt and the Near East.

Finally, about 2,100 years ago, Greece and the rest of Macedonia fell to the Romans. Although many Greek ideas have lived on to the present day, the Romans brought an end to one of the greatest civilizations of all time.

chapter 2

Greek Ideas About Earth and the Universe

α β ψ

This marble tile comes from Miletus, an Ionian colony. It may have once been mounted on the wall of a building.

When Greek city-states became overcrowded about 2,700 years ago, people began to leave what is now mainland Greece in search of new land.

One group settled along the coast of Asia Minor, in an area that is now part of Turkey. The colony that developed eventually became known as Ionia. The Ionians preserved many of the customs and cultural beliefs of the Minoans and Mycenaeans.

Over time, a number of major seaports developed in Ionia. One was Miletus, a bustling trade center. Here both land and sea routes brought together people from Europe, the Middle East, and northern Africa.

The people of Miletus were exposed to the customs and beliefs of many other cultures. As a result, they learned to accept—and even welcome—new ideas. Miletus became the perfect environment for people interested in seeking new

This marble statue shows how Ionian women dressed.

The ruins of Miletus as they appear today

answers to ancient questions about the natural workings of the world. These thinkers also examined human nature, using *logos*, or reason. They refused to accept ideas based on stories or traditions, believing that people should use reason to learn about the world around them.

Thales of Miletus

How was the universe created? What is Earth made of? Is there order in nature? These are the kinds of questions that a man named Thales might have asked. Thales lived in Miletus about 2,600 years ago. He is considered the world's first philosopher of nature.

Thales' ideas flourished among Greek-speaking people. Like other ancient Greek philosophers who followed him, Thales began to separate factual information from opinions and beliefs about creation. Although the word "science" did not exist in Thales' time, he used a strategy similar to the one used by modern scientists. Today, scientists use the *scientific method*—they gather facts, develop an idea or *theory*, perform experiments, and then use the results to draw conclusions.

Greek philosophers collected factual information and developed theories, but they did not conduct experiments. They did, however, write down their ideas about the nature of the universe and how it began. Centuries later, these writings contributed to the growth of science in the rest of Europe.

Thales' Achievements

As a child, Thales became interested in *astronomy* and mathematics. He traveled to Egypt and the Near East to study the stars and learn about *geometry*—a type of math that deals with shapes and the measurement of areas. Legend says that Thales became so absorbed in stargazing that he once fell into a ditch while walking along and staring up at the sky.

In Miletus, Thales founded the Ionian school of natural philosophy. This was the first school to study and develop theories about nature and the origin of Earth. In Thales' view, Earth was flat and floated on an ocean. He thought that the soil, air, and all living things had begun as water and would, over time, change back into water.

A portrait of the Greek philosopher Thales

How did Thales develop such a theory? He probably observed that water appears in three different forms—gas, liquid, and solid. Water changes from one form to another when it is exposed to certain conditions. For example, when ice or snow is heated it becomes liquid water. Thales' idea was probably also based on his understanding that water is necessary for life.

More Ideas About the Universe

Anaximander

Anaximander was an Ionian astronomer who may have been a pupil of Thales. He believed that Earth was a cylinder-shaped planet that had formed from materials that spun off from the universe. The sun, moon, and stars moved in circles around the cylinder.

Anaximander also thought that Earth was suspended within the universe, and that it would rotate freely forever. Over time, Earth's motion had caused the heaviest materials, such as rock, to fall to the center of our planet. Lighter materials, such as water and vapor, rose to the outermost edges of Earth.

Like Thales, Anaximander believed that the first living things spent all their time in the oceans. He claimed that these creatures developed in husks or shells. As time passed, energy from the sun evaporated some of the water that covered Earth, and land appeared. The sea animals found their way to land, shed their husks, and adapted to new ways of life. According to Anaximander, humans evolved from these sea animals. This idea was reintroduced centuries later by Charles Darwin.

Ionian astronomer Anaximander developed ideas about the origin of the universe.

Heraclitus

Other ancient Greek theories about the universe included the idea that fire was the basic element from which all things were created. Heraclitus, who lived in Ephesus about 2,500 years ago, claimed that fire consumes and changes things. He believed that as fire burns, it destroys one thing and creates another. According to Heraclitus, when a solid object burns, a gas forms. This gas can then condense to water.

This idea led Heraclitus to conclude that everything in the universe was in a state of flux, or constant change. In a statement that has been repeated countless times over the ages, he explained, "You can never step twice into the same river." In other words, a river is always changing, so the second time you step into it, it is not the same river.

The Greek philosopher Heraclitus

Anaxagoras

Anaxagoras lived in Athens about 2,400 years ago. He thought that when the universe was created, it separated into two layers and began to rotate. As the whirling motion slowed, stones tore loose from the outer layer

Early Ideas About Atoms

A scientist named Democritus lived about 2,400 years ago in Abdera, a port along the Aegean Sea. Democritus thought that all things are made up of tiny particles called atoms. He said atoms come in a variety of shapes and sizes. Different atoms can combine to form substances with different properties. This idea is very similar to our modern view of the world.

Democritus also claimed that atoms combined to create an infinite number of worlds in the universe. In addition, he believed that the universe itself was made of atoms floating in a vacuum, or void.

In this painting, Democritus is shown with Heraclitus, who is pointing at a globe.

Although most Greeks of the time did not accept Democritus's theories, some of his ideas were preserved. These ancient Greek ideas may have influenced the scientists who lived in the early 1900s as they developed the theories that shape our current understanding of atoms.

Ancient Greek astronomers studied the movements of Earth and the moon.

and fell to Earth as *meteoroids*. This idea was a basis for later studies in *meteorology*.

Anaxagoras correctly concluded that the moon is the closest body to Earth and claimed that it is covered with plains, mountains, and ravines. He understood that the moon reflects light from the sun. He suggested that a *lunar eclipse* occurs when Earth moves between the sun and the moon. He also believed that a *solar eclipse* occurs when the moon moves between the sun and Earth.

Eudoxus

Eudoxus wrote several books on the movements of the sun, moon, and planets. He believed that each of the planets moves through space in a large circle, while simultaneously spinning like a top on its own axis. Some of the astronomical instruments used by modern scientists stem from Eudoxus's theories about the universe. His ideas were also taken into consideration when meteorologists first developed techniques for predicting the weather. Some of these techniques are still used today.

Aristarchus of Samos

Aristarchus of Samos was a Greek who lived in Alexandria, which is now part of Egypt. About 2,300 years ago, he made the first scientific attempt to estimate the size of the sun and the moon, and to calculate their distances from Earth.

Aristarchus of Samos was also the first scientist to suggest that Earth revolves around a stationary sun. This idea was very controversial because most ancient Greeks believed that Earth was at the center of the universe. Although Aristarchus's theory was rejected at the time, centuries later—in 1543—a Polish astronomer named Nicholas Copernicus adopted Aristarchus's ideas. It was not until the early 1600s, however, that other scientists were able to prove that Copernicus and Aristarchus had been correct.

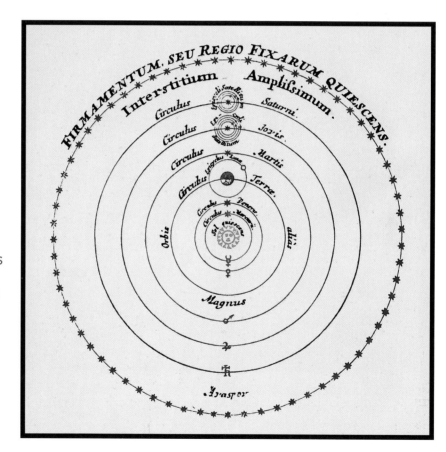

Nicholas Copernicus adopted ideas about the positions of the sun and the planets from the Greek astronomer Aristarchus. This drawing shows how Copernicus envisioned our solar system.

α   β ψ

An artist's interpretation of a model
of the universe proposed by Greek
scholar Claudius Ptolemaeus

After nearly 400 years of thinking about the universe and Earth's place in it, Greek scholars began to realize that certain ideas kept recurring. They began their study by reading the manuscripts left behind by their predecesors. By compiling this information and then adding their own findings, a more solid picture of our world and the rest of the universe began to emerge.

The Greatest Astronomer of Antiquity

Hipparchus of Nicaea was born about 2,190 years ago. He is often referred to as the greatest astronomer of antiquity. As a young man, Hipparchus moved to Rhodes and built an observatory. During his lifetime, he named and cataloged about 850 stars. He was the first person to record the positions of stars using latitude and longitude.

Hipparchus also compiled the records of many earlier astronomers. This allowed him

In this woodcut, Hipparchus is shown studying the night sky from an observatory in Alexandria.

to note changes that had taken place in the sky over a period of 150 years. While making comparisons, he noticed that some stars seemed to change position in relation to certain fixed points in the sky. Hipparchus realized, however, that it was Earth that was moving—not the stars. As Earth orbits around the sun and rotates on its axis, the stars *appear* to move.

Hipparchus was also able to measure the distance of the sun and the moon from Earth more precisely than Aristarchus of Samos. In addition, his theories allowed astronomers in his time, and later, to predict lunar eclipses with extreme accuracy.

Ptolemy Charts the Universe

Claudius Ptolemaeus—better known as Ptolemy—lived from about the year 100 to 170. He based many of his ideas and writings on the research of Hipparchus.

Although he did not accept the idea that Earth moved, he did believe that Earth was a sphere. According to one account, during a sea voyage Ptolemy noticed that a distant island seemed to rise out of the

A painting of Ptolemy done by an Italian artist around 1475.

24

water. He told his companions that Earth's curvature was responsible for this illusion. He also observed that people in different locations saw sunrise at slightly different times. It was always earlier in the east than in the west. This, too, suggested a curved Earth.

Ptolemy was one of the Greek astronomers who disagreed with Aristarchus of Samos. He believed that our planet was at the center of the universe and that all the planets moved around Earth in perfect circles. Ptolemy drew detailed charts to show each planet's movements. Because he was so well respected, Ptolemy convinced the leading scholars of his time that his view of the universe was correct. Even though his charts were often wrong, it took more than 1,400 years for astronomers to prove that the sun—not Earth—is at the center of our solar system.

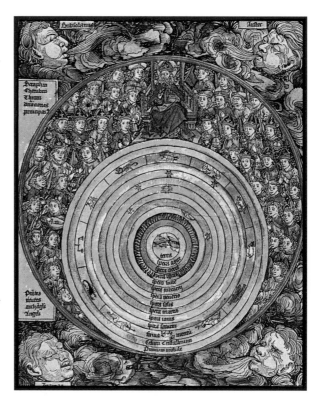

This engraving, which was completed in 1493, is another interpretation of how Ptolemy envisioned the universe. Compare it to the image on page 22.

Ptolemy's writings also include descriptions of his experiments with optics and how light rays refract—seem to bend—when passing from one medium to another. In a book entitled *Optics*, Ptolemy explained how starlight is refracted by the atmosphere, making a star appear to be higher in the sky than it really is.

Ptolemy's greatest achievement was a thirteen-volume text that became known as the *Almagest*, meaning "the greatest." The *Almagest* brought together the most important findings of Greek astronomers and expanded the catalog of stars.

An Astronomer's Tools

The *Almagest* included descriptions of instruments commonly used by astronomers. One device was a block of wood with an eyehole. The block slid back and forth in a wooden frame and was used to determine the width of the sun's disk.

Greek astronomers also used a tool called a *gnomon*. (The word "gnomon" comes from a Greek word meaning "one who knows.") A gnomon is a pole or stake that is placed in the ground in an open, flat area. The pole casts a shadow from sunrise to sunset. In the early morning, the shadow is very long. As the morning passes and the sun rises in the sky, the shadow becomes shorter and shorter. The shadow is shortest when the sun reaches its highest point in the sky. Greek observers called this time of day "real" noon. As the afternoon passes, a gnomon's shadow grows longer and longer until the sun sets.

Besides telling Greeks the time of day, gnomons also helped astronomers determine the time of year. By watching the gnomon over time, the Greeks could observe when the *solstices*—the longest and shortest days of the year—occurred.

Gnomon

Shadow

Greek scientists used gnomons to tell the time of day. Here, a scientist and his student note that the days are growing shorter

This information allowed Greek astronomers to calculate when the sun would cross the equator. This happens twice each year—once in March and once in September. On days when the center of the sun is directly over the equator, there are exactly 12 hours of daylight and 12 hours of darkness. These days are called *equinoxes*. This term is a combination of Latin words meaning "equal night."

The Greeks kept careful records of the sun's position during each equinox. By the year 100, they noticed that the sun does not always pass

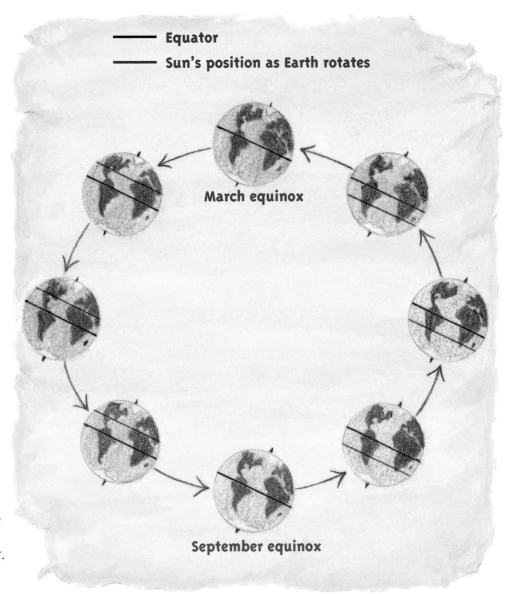

Equator

Sun's position as Earth rotates

March equinox

September equinox

The equinoxes are the two days of the year when the sun crosses the equator.

over the same point along the equator. Eventually, scientists realized that the gravitational pull of the moon and the sun causes Earth to wobble slightly, like a top that is spinning on a table.

From Astronomy to Geography

Geography—the study and description of Earth's surfaces—owes a great debt to Greek astronomers. Many of the measuring techniques originally developed to determine the size of the sun and moon and to calculate the distances of these objects from Earth could also be used to measure the heights of mountains, the depths of valleys, and the *volumes* of lakes.

As astronomers recorded the positions of more and more stars, mapmakers began to locate places on Earth by finding their positions relative to certain stars. Using this information, the mapmakers then determined each site's longitude and latitude.

Ptolemy is remembered for bringing astronomy and geography together. He wrote a major text called *Geography*, which listed about 8,000 places—cities and other sites. The book also contains maps and charts that show how to represent the curved Earth on a flat surface.

This world map is based on information taken from *Geography* by Claudius Ptolemaeus.

chapter 4
Mathematicians in Ancient Greece

The Greek mathematician
Pythagoras studied geometry as well
as the relationship between math
and patterns found in nature.

Geometry

The main focus of ancient Greek mathematics was geometry. The word "geometry" comes from two Greek words meaning "Earth" and "to measure." Geometry began as a system of rules for measuring areas on Earth. Today, it is considered an advanced branch of mathematics.

The Greeks learned some very basic rules of geometry from the Egyptians. Over the centuries, the Egyptians had developed a number of methods for measuring *area*. Egyptian farmers measured plots of farmland in order to figure out how much seed they needed to buy. Egyptian builders measured areas of land before they planned the layout of cities. The Greeks learned how the Egyptians measured distances and heights, and then developed new, improved methods of their own.

The Pythagoreans

A famous Greek mathematician named Pythagoras lived about 2,500 years ago. He was born on the island of Samos and eventually settled in Crotona, which is now in southern Italy.

Pythagoras set up a school for men and women. His students—known as the Pythagorean Order—dressed and ate simply. They believed the mind could be purified through scientific study, and spent most of their time developing mathematical theories.

This illustration depicts Pythagoras teaching at his school.

According to one of these theories, "all things are numbers." This idea may have something to do with the close relationship between mathematics and the patterns found in nature, music, and the orbits of the planets.

In music, Pythagoreans observed, notes on the scale correspond to the lengths of vibrating strings or vibrating columns of air. Plucking one string of a guitar will produce a note. If that string is cut in half, the note will be an octave, or eight tones, higher.

Pythagoreans were probably the first people to try to understand the physical makeup of objects in terms of numbers and measurements. Their ideas about mathematical relationships still influence scientific thinking.

A young man plays a lyre, a musical instrument that could have helped Pythagoras develop theories about the relationship between patterns in music and in math.

What Euclid Gave Us

The study of mathematics continued to develop and flourish for the next few centuries. About 2,200 years ago, a mathematician and physicist named Euclid studied in Athens, and then in Alexandria. Euclid wrote numerous math—or geometry—textbooks. One of his most important works was called *Elements*. This text has been the basis for teaching geometry for more than 2,000 years.

Euclid also spent time teaching a few dedicated students. One of his students was a Greek king who wanted to find a quick, easy way to learn math. The king did not want to work step by step through all the volumes that made up the *Elements*. Euclid told the king that "there is no royal road to learning." In other words, all people—even kings—had to follow the same difficult path, if they wanted to master mathematics.

This page from Euclid's book *Elements* was reproduced in the twelfth century.

Eratosthenes' Experiment

Eratosthenes was another famous Greek mathematician who lived in Alexandria about 2,200 years ago. One of Eratosthenes' most important accomplishments was calculating the *circumference* of Earth (the distance around Earth at its widest point).

Eratosthenes had read that in the town of Syene, which was south of Alexandria, the sun lit up the bottom of a deep well on only one day of the year. This happened at midday on June 21 (the summer solstice), when the sun was directly overhead. Eratosthenes looked at the records kept by astronomers who carefully watched a gnomon in Alexandria. He found that the sun was never directly overhead at noon on June 21 in Alexandria. Eratosthenes concluded that he could use this information to measure Earth's circumference.

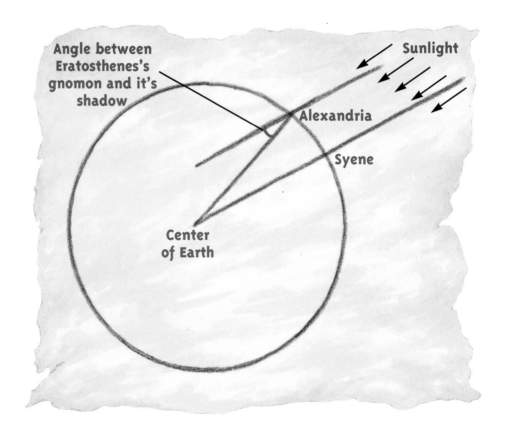

Angle between Eratosthenes's gnomon and it's shadow

Sunlight

Alexandria

Syene

Center of Earth

To calculate Earth's circumference, Eratosthene measured the angle between a gnomon and its shadow at midday on June 21. Because Eratosthene knew the distance between Syene and Alexandria and that there are 360 degrees in a circle, he was able to find the circumference of the Earth.

He placed one gnomon in the ground in Syene and another in the ground in Alexandria. On the next summer solstice, Eratosthenes measured the angle of the gnomon's shadow in Alexandria. He theorized that, since Earth is a sphere, the angle of the gnomon's shadow would be equal to the angle between Alexandria and Syene. Using this angle measurement and the distance between Alexandria and Syene, Eratosthenes calculated the distance around Earth. His estimate was close to the value scientists accept today—24,860 miles (40,008 km).

Using his circumference measurement, Eratosthenes also calculated the *diameter* of Earth (the distance across). This estimate, too, was very close to the accepted value of about 7,900 miles (12,714 km).

Even today, students in schools across the United States duplicate Eratosthenes's experiment. Instructions for these activities are available on the Internet, so that people around the world have access to them.

More Mathematical Studies

Hippocrates of Chios is remembered for his effort to develop a formula for finding the dimensions of the square that is equal in area to a specific circle. Although he was unable to solve this problem, he did discover the area of a shape called a *lune*.

The work of Hippocrates influenced later mathematicians, such as

A lune is the shape created when two circles overlap.

The Greek mathematician Hypatia was the head of a school in Alexandria.

Apollonius, who searched for ways to measure curves and find the areas of cones. Apollonius wrote *On Conics*, a book that explained the properties of the curves that result when a cone is divided by a straight line. Hundreds of years later, understanding these curves helped European mathematicians develop theories about the *orbits* of the planets.

Apollonius's work also influenced Hypatia of Alexandria—the first Greek woman to make significant contributions to mathematics. She lived during the late 300s and early 400s and was the head of a school in Alexandria. She expanded on Appollonius's theories and wrote commentaries on the work of various Greek mathematicians. Unfortunately, only a few references to her writings remain. Most of her ideas were lost after her death.

chapter 5

How Ancient Greeks Healed the Sick

This relief shows a Greek healer treating a patient.

The very early Greeks thought illness was a punishment inflicted by the gods. Diseases were treated with herbal concoctions, special diets, exercise, and sometimes *bloodletting*. The ancient Greeks often used expressions like, "Time is the great physician." This medical advice has some value. Even today, we often say, "Time heals all wounds."

Knowledge of *anatomy* and *physiology*—the makeup of the body and how it works—was also limited. Ancient Greeks did not study body organs because dissecting—cutting open—human corpses might offend the gods.

Bleeding a patient was common treatment in ancient Greece.

Early Greek scientists did, however, have some knowledge of the human body's bone and muscle structure. This information came primarily from treating athletic injuries—sprains, bone fractures, and dislocations—at Greek gymnasiums.

Ancient Greeks gained information about the body's structure by treating athletes who worked out in gymnasiums.

The ancient Greeks also knew how to treat wounded soldiers. Some of the earliest descriptions of battlefield surgery and the use of anesthetics appear in the *Iliad*, a long poem by a Greek poet named Homer. The *Iliad* describes a war between the Greeks and the people of Troy, which was located on the coast of Asia Minor.

Medical Schools and Practice

A little more than 2,000 years ago, some progress was made in Greek medical science. Pericles, the ruler of Athens, encouraged his people to set up four schools of medicine. Hippocrates founded one of these schools on the island of Cos, which is off the coast of what is now Turkey.

Hippocrates, and those who studied at his school, rejected traditional views of disease. *Hippocratic Corpus,* a collection of writings by Hippocrates and his later followers, stressed the importance of looking for rational causes for disease. One essay, for example, argues against the idea that a person with a disease like *epilepsy* is possessed by demons. The writer declared that all illnesses are the result of natural causes or *heredity.*

The Hippocratic school made a major contribution to medicine by setting standards for doctors. These were spelled out in the Hippocratic

An engraving of the Greek physician Hippocrates

oath, which has been a guide for medical practitioners for more than 2,000 years. By taking the oath, a physician promises to be honest with patients, to protect and preserve life, and to keep information about patients private.

Understanding Anatomy and Disease

Several centuries after Hippocrates' time, Greek medical scientists in Alexandria began a systematic study of anatomy. Because Greek healers no longer feared the anger of the gods, they routinely dissected bodies.

Ancient physicians Herophilus and Erasistratus

Herophilus was an anatomist who developed a number of useful techniques for dissecting corpses. He described and named many of the organs he found in the human body. For example, he carefully explained the makeup of the brain and understood that the brain is the center of the nervous system.

Erasistratus, another anatomist, continued the work of Herophilus. But Erasistratus was more interested in searching for the causes of diseases. He routinely dissected the bodies of people who had just died. These *autopsies* revealed injuries to or changes in the bodies' organs that helped him determine why the patients had died.

Animal and Plant Research

Animal research also aided physicians in their medical studies. The great philosopher Aristotle carefully observed and investigated many types of animals. He wrote several books describing the body structures of various

This painting depicts Aristotle describing animals.

animals. He also explained how certain land and sea animals function and reproduce. Many of his findings are recorded in *History of Animals*, which contains detailed descriptions that compare favorably to present-day studies.

Aristotle also conducted important experiments on developing chicks. Aristotle instructed students: "Take twenty or more eggs and let them be incubated by two or more hens. Then each day, from the second. . . remove an egg, break it, and examine it." By the tenth day, "the chick and all its parts are visible," he explained. Aristotle compared the chick with the human *embryo*, noting that the chick lies in the egg "in the same way the infant lies within its mother's womb."

In ancient Greece, plants—especially herbs— were used to treat many illnesses.

In ancient Greece, physicians also depended on the use of various plants, particularly herbs, to aid in the healing process or to reduce or prevent pain. Numerous studies focused on toxic, or poisonous, plants. Accidental or deliberate death by poisoning was common in ancient Greece, so physicians needed to find herbal potions that would counteract poisoning.

Bringing Information Together

Centuries passed before the various findings of Greek medical and biological scientists were compiled for practical use. Galen, a Greek surgeon who lived about 2,000 years ago in Rome, Italy, collected information about earlier Greek achievements.

Galen studied at the medical school in Alexandria. Later, he conducted experiments and developed his own theories. Eventually, he came up with a model that explained the way organs and other parts of the human body function. He was the first to suggest that blood—not air —flows through the arteries.

Galen wrote several hundred texts on medical science. His books, which included his own findings as well as those of earlier scientists, were translated into several languages. The ideas that Galen compiled became a basis for medical theories developed by later physicians and anatomists.

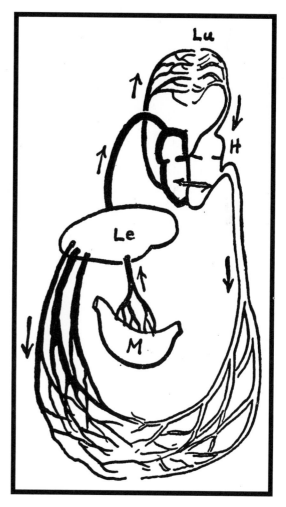

This diagram shows Galen's ideas about how blood flows through the body. (Lu = the lungs, H = the heart, Le = the liver, M = the stomach)

chapter 6

Applying Science

Plato and his students

The study of "pure" science was considered noble in ancient Greece. But many early Greeks had no interest in applied science—using knowledge about how nature works to make machines, household devices, and other useful items. Philosophers and other thinkers were expected to use their minds, not their hands, in their life's work.

A marble sculpture of Socrates, one of the greatest philosophers of the ancient world

The great philosopher Socrates of Athens, who lived a little more than 2,000 years ago, was even against the study of the physical world. He was more concerned about moral values than about how nature worked. Socrates influenced many Greek thinkers, including his most famous student, Plato. Plato criticized mathematicians who experimented with mechanical devices. He thought mechanics was a "corruption" of geometry.

Nevertheless, Plato's friend Archytas, who was a mathematician, worked on mechanical inventions. He is said to have invented the screw and the pulley, which were vital for the development of the machine industry centuries later.

The Legendary Archimedes

About 2,300 years ago, some Greek scientists began exploring the relationships between mathematics and machinery. Archimedes was one of

An ingraving of the Greek scientist Archimedes

the greatest figures in Greek mathematics and mechanics at this time. He lived most of his 75 years in Syracuse, which was on the island of Sicily, and probably studied for a time in Alexandria.

Archimedes wanted to be remembered for his work in mathematics. In fact, one of his geometrical formulas was engraved on his tombstone. He calculated the value of pi (π) with greater accuracy than anyone before him. Pi is the ratio of the circumference of a circle to its diameter. Archimedes claimed that the value of pi is greater than $3\frac{10}{17}$ but less than $3\frac{1}{7}$. Today, geometry students know that pi is approximately 3.1416, which is very close to $3\frac{1}{7}$.

Many legends surround Archimedes' work. One of the most widely told stories describes his discovery of the *density* of fluids.

Apparently, Hieron, the king of Syracuse, wanted to know whether his crown was made of solid gold. The king suspected that the metalsmith who made the crown had cheated him. The king had provided the metalsmith with a large piece of gold. To make the crown, the metalsmith had to melt down the gold and then shape it into a crown. The king was afraid that the metalsmith had mixed some of the gold with silver—a less valuable metal—and kept some of the pure gold for himself.

It was impossible to melt the crown to determine the metal content, so Archimedes had to find another way to solve the problem. Supposedly, Archimedes discovered the answer while at a public bath.

Archimedes studies a mathematical problem.

When he climbed into the water, the tub overflowed. By measuring the amount of overflow, he found that the volume of the spilled water was equal to the volume of his body under water.

Archimedes realized he could use this principle to measure the amount of gold in the king's crown. If the crown was solid gold, it would *displace* the same amount of water as a lump of gold with the same weight as the crown. A specific volume of silver weighs more than the same volume of gold. So if the metalsmith had mixed in silver, the crown would weigh more the gold lump.

Archimedes was supposedly so excited by his idea that he jumped out of the tub and ran naked down the street, shouting "EUREKA!"—a phrase that means "I have found it!"

If you look carefully at this ancient artifact, you will see that it depicts a man using an Archimedes' screw.

When Archimedes tested the crown, he discovered that the crown was not made of pure gold. The metalsmith had tried to cheat the king by replacing some of the gold with silver.

This legend focuses on the fact that Archimedes was the first person to develop a physical law that explains why objects seem to lose weight in water or other liquids.

Although he was a renowned mathematician, Archimedes also became known for his mechanical inventions. He constructed movable spheres and other shapes to work through mechanical problems. He also built a kind of *planetarium* with movable parts representing the sun, moon, and planets. They all circled a bronze ball that represented Earth.

Archimedes' most important invention is what is now known as Archimedes' screw, a device used to move water from a lower level to a higher level. It consists of a spiral-like pipe inside a cylinder. When the pipe rotates, water moves upward. This device is still used in some developing countries where other types of pumps are not available.

Was Archimedes Right?

According to Archimedes, when an object floats on—or is submerged in—a fluid, it is held up by a force equal to the weight of the fluid that is displaced by the object. To determine whether Archimedes was right, try the following experiment.

You will need a food or postage scale, a small plastic container with a watertight cover (such as one that contained spices, party tooth-picks, or medication), a measuring cup that holds 2 to 4 cups (480 to 960 mL) of material and has markings for volume (cups or milliliters) as well as weight (ounces or grams), a pencil, and a notebook. *Be sure to conduct this experiment in a sink.*

1. Add at least 1 cup (240 mL) of water to the measuring cup. Record the exact volume and weight of the water in the notebook.

2. Fill the plastic container with water and place the lid on secure-ly. Weigh the plastic container on the scale, and record this value in the notebook.

3. Put the plastic container in the measuring cup and note how much water it displaces. Write these results (volume and weight) in the notebook, too.

4. Compare the weight of the plastic container (Step 2) to the weight of the water you measured (Step 3). Your plastic con-tainer should weigh the same amount as the displaced water.

5. Try the experiment again, packing the plastic container with a material such as sand, pebbles, marbles, buttons, or beads. Do you get the same results?

Each time the plastic container is placed in the measuring cup, it should displace water that is equal to the weight of the container. If the filled container is lighter than the surrounding water, it will rise or float. If the filled container is heavier than the surrounding water, it will sink.

Other Greek Inventions

Ctesibius

Ctesibius, who lived around 2,200 years ago, is remembered for explaining the properties of air as it moves through a tube. Strange as it seems, Ctesibius did his work in a barbershop. He discovered these properties while inventing an adjustable mirror for his father, who was a barber.

A system of pulleys and a lead weight could be used to move the mirror up and down. The pulley cord and weight were inside a long tube. When the cord was pulled, the weight dropped. As the weight fell, air was pushed out of the tube, creating a loud musical noise. A design very similar to the one developed by Ctesibius is now used to make springs for some doors.

Philon of Byzantium

Archimedes was not the only Greek scholar who used scientific knowledge to create useful devices. Gadgets were the specialty of Philon of Byzantium. Among his clever devices were "trick pitchers" with metal figures that performed acrobatics when water was poured out. He also designed cups with false bottoms that seemed to go dry when liquid was poured into them. He even created mechanical washbasins that operated with pulleys and weights.

One elaborate production was a bronze hand that held a *pumice* stone, which was used like soap. When a person took the pumice, the bronze hand withdrew, and water flowed for washing. After a few moments, the

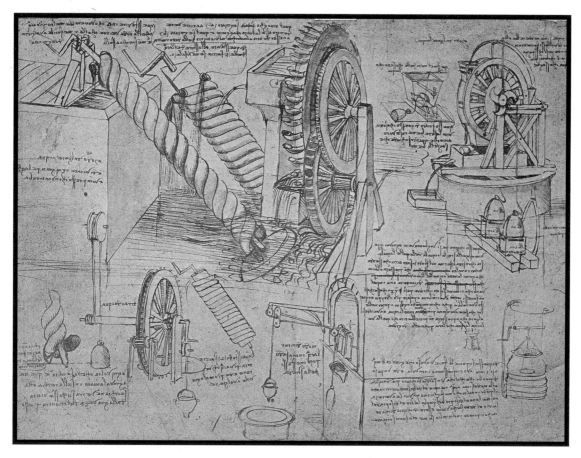

Leonardo da Vinci, an Italian scientist and artist who lived in the 1500s, sketched all sorts of ideas in his notebook. This page shows a variety of Archimedes' screws and waterwheels.

water stopped and the hand appeared again to offer the bather another pumice stone.

Philon also invented practical devices. One was a mechanism in which a waterwheel was used to fill and lift buckets of stream water. A similar technology was used later in grain mills.

Heron used steam to propel some of his gadgets.

Heron of Alexandria

Heron of Alexandria was another mechanical wizard. He was known for his work in optics. Heron invented an instrument called a dioptra, which was used by surveyors to measure angles. One of his most playful inventions was a miniature theater with automated dancers on turntables.

Heron also developed a revolving globe. When he mounted the globe on tubes that were connected to a small boiler, steam from the boiler pushed the globe around. This may have been the first mechanism to use a kind of jet propulsion.

Although Heron and other ancient Greeks produced many fanciful devices and mechanical instruments, their inventions probably had a more serious purpose. Ancient mechanical "wizards" often built such gadgets to prove their mathematical principles and theories.

chapter 7

The Ancient Greek Heritage

This painting, completed in 1510 by Italian artist Raphael, shows the great scholars of ancient Greece. Plato and Socrates are in the middle. Pythagoras is on the right.

Greek ideas and ways of life spread far and wide, but over the centuries wars between city-states and against foreign empires took their toll.

Although Greek lands eventually became part of the Roman Empire, Greek ideas and accomplishments were not lost. The Romans were greatly influenced by the vast treasury of Greek knowledge. Unlike the Greeks, the Romans did not hesitate to apply science. They used physical principles developed by Greek scientists to build walls, roads, aqueducts, harbors, and many other public facilities. The Romans passed on Greek learning by absorbing and adapting it.

Romans applied what Greek scientists had learned about the world and mathematics to construct bridges, aqueducts, and arenas. Many of the Romans' greatest structures—including this aqueduct—still stand today.

As the Roman Empire expanded, Greek culture spread. Greek ideas even survived the fall of the Roman Empire in 476. Scholars in the Arab-speaking world collected, analyzed, and expanded on the scientific knowledge accumulated by the Greeks and Romans. Eventually, this same information was rediscovered by European scientists who lived during the Renaissance.

Modern science benefits from the methodical research techniques developed by the Greeks. Greek scholars also passed on their love of learning, respect for wisdom, and interest in the diligent search for truth. Perhaps ancient Greece's most important contribution to science was the emphasis it placed on rational inquiry. This attitude has been carried across time and continues to influence us today.

After Rome fell, Muslim armies swept through northern Africa and parts of Europe. They collected and learned from ancient manuscripts written by scholars such as Aristotle, who is depicted in this illustration.

GLOSSARY

anatomy—the study of an organism's body structure.

area—the amount of space that falls within an established set of lines.

astronomy—the study of objects outside Earth's atmosphere.

autopsy—the examination of a dead body. An autopsy is done to determine the cause of death or to study how a disease has affected the body.

bloodletting—allowing a person to bleed. In the past, some healers believed that removing some blood from the body could cure some diseases.

circumference—the distance around the widest part of Earth or another spherical object.

civilization—the culture of people living in a particular area during a specific period of time.

democracy—a system of government in which all citizens make decisions.

density—the mass of an object per unit volume. When the object is placed in a liquid, its density can be determined by the amount of fluid it displaces.

diameter—the distance across a circle.

displace—to move out of the way.

embryo—a human or creature in the very early stages of development.

epilepsy—a disease of the central nervous system. People with this condition experience periodic seizures.

equinox—the two times of the year (in March and September) when the sun is over the equator and day and night are exactly equal in length.

geometry—a branch of mathematics that deals with the measurement of areas and the relationships between shapes.

gnomon—a vertical pole used to measure the angle of the sun by the shadow it casts.

heredity—having to do with genetic traits that are passed from parent to child.

lunar eclipse—when the moon is hidden by a shadow cast by Earth as it moves between the sun and moon.

lune—the shape of the overlapping area between two adjacent circles.

meteoroid—a particle of dust or rock that enters Earth's atmosphere.

meteorology—the study of weather patterns and climate.

orbit—a circular path, such as that made by Earth around the sun.

physiology—the study of an organism's body functions.

planetarium—a model of the solar system.

pumice—a type of lightweight volcanic glass that is full of small holes. It is sometimes used to remove layers of dead skin.

scientific method—a system of investigation.

solar eclipse—when the moon moves between Earth and the sun.

solstice—the longest and shortest days of the year. In the Northern Hemisphere, the summer solstice usually occurs on June 22 and the winter solstice on December 22.

theory—a set of principles or ideas proposed to explain a particular event or situation.

volume—the amount of space occupied by an object.

RESOURCES

Books

Cohen, Daniel. *Ancient Greece*. New York: Doubleday, 1990.

Descamps-Lequine, Sophie. *The Ancient Greeks: In the Land of the Gods*. Brookfield, CT: Millbrook Press, 1992.

Ipsen, D.C. *Archimedes: Greatest Scientist of the Ancient World*. Hillside, NJ: Enslow, 1988.

Keller, Mary Jo. *Ancient Greece Activity Book: Arts, Crafts, Cooking, Historical Aids*. San Juan Capistrano, CA: Edupress, 1995.

Kerr, Daisy. *Ancient Greeks*. Danbury, CT: Franklin Watts, 1996.

Lafferty, Peter. *Archimedes*. New York: Bookwright, 1991.

Lasky, Kathryn. *The Librarian Who Measured the Earth*. Boston: Little, Brown, 1994.

Macdonald, Fiona. *I Wonder Why Greeks Built Temples & Other Questions About Ancient Greece*. New York: Larousse Kingfisher Chambers, 1997.

Nardo, Don. *Life in Ancient Greece*. San Diego: Lucent Books, 1996.

Odijk, Pamela. *The Greeks*. Englewood Cliffs, NJ: Silver Burdett Press, 1989.

Purdy, Susan Gold and Cass R. Sandak. *Ancient Greece*. New York: Franklin Watts, 1982.

Simon, Charnan. *Explorers of the Ancient World*. Chicago: Children's Press, 1990.

Internet Sites

Due to the changeable nature of the Internet, sites appear and disappear very quickly. The following resources offered useful information on ancient civilizations at the time of publication.

Ancient World Web provides descriptions of many Web sites that have information about ancient civilizations. Its address is
http://atlantic.evsc.virginia.edu/julia/AncientWorld.html.

East Middle School's Ancient Culture Page provides information about many of the world's ancient civilizations. You can learn about the ancient Greeks, Romans, Chinese, and Mayans at
http://www.macatawa.org/org/ems/anccult.html.

Exploring Ancient World Culture includes maps, timelines, essays, and images that describe ancient civilizations in Rome, China, Greece, and the Near East. It can be reached at
http://eawc.evansville.edu/index.htm.

Measuring the Solar System is just one of many Internet sites that describes how Eratosthenes calculated the circumference of Earth. The address for this site is
http://www.phys.virginia.edu/classes/109N/lectures/gkastr1.html.

INDEX

ABOUT THE AUTHOR

Kathlyn Gay is the author of more than ninety books. Some of her most recent works have been done in collaboration with family members. Many of Kathlyn's books focus on environmental and social issues, history, and culture. She has written sixteen books for Franklin Watts, including several award winners. Kathlyn and her husband, Arthur Gay, live in Zion, Illinois.